re:ac

# Chosen for change

## am I part of God's big plan?

### Kate Hayes

**small group Bible resources from
Scripture Union**

**CHOSEN FOR CHANGE**

Published by Scripture Union, 207–209 Queensway, Bletchley, MK2 2EB, England.

Scripture Union: We are an international Christian charity working with churches in more than 130 countries providing resources to bring the good news about Jesus Christ to children, young people and families – and to encourage them to develop spiritually through the Bible and prayer. As well as our network of volunteers, staff and associates who run holidays, church-based events and school Christian groups, we produce a wide range of publications and support those who use our resources through training programmes.

Email: info@scriptureunion.org.uk
Internet: http://www.scriptureunion.org.uk

First published 2002

ISBN 1 85999 623 X

Scripture taken from the *New Living Translation*, British text, published by Tyndale House Publishers, Inc, Wheaton, Illinois, USA, and distributed by STL Ltd, Carlisle, Cumbria, England; and from *The Message* © Eugene H Peterson, used by permission of NavPress Publishing Group.

British Library Cataloguing-in-Publication Data: a catalogue record for this book is available from the British Library.

Cover design and photography by David Lund Design, Milton Keynes.

Illustrations by Helen Gale.

Printed and bound in Great Britain by Ebenezer Baylis & Son Ltd, The Trinity Press, London Road, Worcester WR5 2JH.

# Contents

# Welcome!

Welcome to **re:action** discussion guides for small groups!

What are the distinctives of **re:action**? The series is strong on links into the contemporary world and concerned that God's Word impacts our everyday lives in practical ways. Understanding the truth leads to a response in the heart and mind of the individual. The sessions encourage personal discovery through actively exploring the Bible but, unlike many group Bible studies on the market, **re:action** assumes little if any prior Bible knowledge. As such it is excellent for those new to looking at Christianity, but that is not to say that the series is lightweight or lacking in depth. More mature Christians will find the series refreshing. The quality of questions should produce lively and thinking debate, and opportunities to share personal experiences. Though some humour is used, especially in the icebreaker **set the scene** sections, the content of the sessions overall is demanding and personally challenging.

Kate Hayes began writing the series out of a sense of frustration with existing materials, and everything she produces has been tried and tested in her own church groups. She says: 'Most study notes are frankly boring. Too many work on a 'the answer must be Jesus' principle, regurgitating bits of text for answers. Others don't seem to relate the learning so as to make a difference to people's everyday lives. I don't write these notes because I want people to find answers to academic questions or clock up the books they've studied and then move on to something else, but because I want to see people grow in understanding and maturity. I want them to find out things that will make a difference every day of their lives, when work is tough, when friends let them down, their lives fall apart and they're faced with living as Christians in our postmodern society.'

Each title in the series contains material for seven sessions. **Preview** is an introductory session that ideally would take place in a social setting, perhaps following a potluck supper or around desserts and coffee. Each session begins with **set the scene**, a light discussion opener, sometimes in the form of a quiz or game, or some fun questions. The **explore** section takes the group into the Bible text, while the **reflect** section moves into the area of personal application. Note that while most of the questions are for group discussion, there are also periods of quiet for tackling personal questions, which don't have to be shared more widely. In the closing **re:action** section there is opportunity to pray through what's been discussed and discovered, and sometimes suggestions for other actions both within and outside the group times.

What about leadership of the group? The **re:action** series is aimed at thinking people willing to be pro-active in searching the Scriptures and discussing their implications. As such, the leadership of the group, by one or two members, can be run with a light touch. The role of the **re:action** group leader is that of a guide through the discussion material rather than a teacher. The leader will sensitively encourage the sharing of answers and personal experiences at an appropriate level. Many questions need just one word answers and can be moved through quite quickly; at other times some brainstorming of ideas would be an appropriate response to the questions; sometimes it will be a more measured and thoughtful discussion. The leader will need to make decisions about when tangents to the discussion are legitimate and when they distract.

Ideally everyone should have their own copy of the booklet and follow through the material together. It's essential for everyone to bring a Bible, as much of the time will be spent around open Bibles. Any translation is fine, and it's often useful to compare different versions. For those new to Bible study, several contemporary translations are to be recommended: the Good News Bible, the Contemporary English Version, or the New Living Translation – and it's the NLT which is used in the booklet whenever Bible text is quoted. It will be useful to have a supply of pens, paper and perhaps card available.

## About the author

Kate Hayes, born into a non-churchgoing family in Sheffield, decided to become a Christian aged 12 after being 'dragged along' to a Pathfinder meeting by a friend. After studying Psychology she did teacher training but then found herself working in bookshops and in software testing for the book trade. In 1994 she moved to Dukinfield in Greater Manchester, where she now coordinates and writes materials for small groups in St John's Church.

# Intro

Jemima and Flo are the church pew-polishing team. One day Flo sees a mega pew-polishing machine, which is much quicker and more effective than spit and cloth and buys it on the spot. However, she fails to consult Jemima first, and when Jemima finds out she storms off in a huff. Although Jemima later returns to the polishing team she moans about Flo's actions to others and downplays how good the machine is.

In church on Sunday, as well as Flo and Jemima, there are others who aren't so happy either. There's Rebecca, who's upset that Jenny didn't speak to her last week and so she's ignoring her this week. Simon's annoyed that nobody asked him personally to help tidy up the church grounds (although it was on the notice sheet as a general request) so he won't turn up for that. And Basil is so fed up that his suggestions as part of the hymnbook-purchasing committee were over-ruled, he's since refused to be part of the chalice-buying group as well.

Funny stories… the stuff of sitcom and comedy sketch. But also the stuff of real life. There's often a great gulf fixed between our commitment to Christ and our behaviour in everyday life. We know we should love and respect others, and do it without exception – but when our toes get trodden on we're likely to over-react. We know that peace and reconciliation should be hallmarks of the Christian – but when our neighbour's cat digs up our rosebeds, we have a tendency to forget. We know our language should be clean and encouraging – but when the clever cutting remark is on the tip of our tongue we somehow can't resist coming out with it. We know that all we do, say and think should reflect the standards of the kingdom, should demonstrate that we are changed people in Christ – but it's all too easy to get complacent and slip back into old ways. We know we should be acutely aware of the spiritual battle raging in our world – but it's sometimes more comfortable to slip back from the front line and take a nap in the trenches.

No more 'buts'! Let's look for some insights and advice that are both godly and practical. We're going to learn from a letter written by amazing early Christian leader Paul to some of the Christians at a place called Ephesus, whose problems sound all too familiar despite the distances of time and geography.

# 1 Preview

*Long ago... God loved us and chose us in Christ...*

**Ephesians 1:4**

## set the scene

You have a quiet evening in ahead of you. All your important jobs are done and you're planning to relax. Which one of these options would you choose?

- a new book by your favourite author
- the video you recorded of your favourite programme
- assembling that new pine bookcase

You get stuck in and soon you're having a great time! BUT THEN...

- due to a printing error, the last chapter is missing!
- the TV goes wonky and you can't watch the last ten minutes!
- two vital screws go missing and it won't stand up!

Q: How do you feel now?

Q: Why do you feel like this?

Q: What do you do? Can you recall the last time you experienced this kind of frustration? Describe it to the group.

**Reality check** When these things were created (the novel, the TV programme, the furniture flatpack) they were made to be watched or read or used as a whole – not with bits missing. Each piece has a crucial part to play in the finished product.

# 1 God's choice

**Read**

Ephesians 1:1–14

Imagine you are in the supermarket buying a packet of biscuits for yourself.

Q: What things do you consider before making your choice?


Q: Would you have chosen the same biscuits if you were about to entertain 20 teenagers from the youth group?


Q: Or to eat on a long walk on a hot day?


We choose things with their eventual purpose in mind. If...

- we're dieting we probably won't buy high calorie, high fat toffee-filled bars
- we're unadventurous we probably won't try those new Vindaloo Digestives
- we're broke we might prefer the supermarket's own brand custard creams to the fancy chocolate things that are two for £1.99

God chose us with a purpose in mind too.

Q: What, as revealed in Ephesians, is his purpose for the world?


Q: How can I be sure that everyone who trusts in Jesus has a part to play in this purpose? Take a closer look at these verses and put your suggested answers against them.
  v4
  v5
  v11

Everyone who loves and serves Jesus can be sure they have been **chosen** to be part of God's family.

Q: How do you feel about God choosing you?

In some versions of the Bible the wording used has Paul describing us not just as **chosen** (v4,11) but as **predestined** (v5,11).

Predestination is an idea that people have struggled to understand for centuries and still argue about today. Note that the emphasis is on God's love (v4). We shouldn't get hung up on matters we can't be sure about, but be glad that all who belong to Christ are incredibly blessed because of God's all-conquering love. Of course, the fact that God chooses believers doesn't take away from our own responsibility to make the decision to follow Christ.

## 2 Our choice

**Read**

2 Peter 3:8–10

Q: Think back to a time when you were offered a job, a place on a course or membership of a group. How did you feel at being chosen in this way?

Q: Have you ever turned down such an offer/invitation? Why/why not?

reflect

For some, hearing and believing the good news about Jesus happens at the same moment. For others these events may happen many years apart.

Q: When did you first **hear** the gospel?

Q: When did you first **believe** it?

Q: What made you take the step from hearing to believing?

If we are to play our part in God's plans then we need help.

**Read**
Ephesians 1:15–23

Q: What does Paul pray his readers will receive? (v17–19)

Q: What benefits will these things bring them?

Q: What kinds of things do you usually include in your prayers for others?

Q: Why do you think Paul doesn't pray for the personal needs and practical problems his readers face?

## re:action

Share any personal needs you might have with the group so that you can all **pray** for each other. Begin your time of prayer with one person **reading** out this simplified version of Ephesians 1:17:

*I pray that God would give you spiritual wisdom and understanding, so that you might grow in your knowledge of God.*

Then go round the group, each person in turn saying, 'we pray for…' ending with the name of the person on their left. Spend a short time praying for that person either aloud or in silence, as you prefer, then move on.

On a piece of card or paper (postcard size would be about right), **write** out the verse and add below the names of everyone in the group. **Take** the card home with you and keep somewhere you'll see it regularly. Over the next few days **pray** this prayer for the members of your group in turn, replacing 'you' with their name.

Before your next meeting you will find it helpful to **read** through the book of Ephesians in a contemporary translation such as the *New International Version*, the *Good News Bible*, the *Contemporary English Version* or the *New Living Translation*. Or try *The Message* – a paraphrase rather than a translation – written by American Eugene H Peterson.

# 2  Brought together

*For Christ himself has made peace between us...*

**Ephesians 2:14**

## set the scene

Start by playing a short game together that involves two teams, such as charades, a quiz or even cricket – depending on how active you're all feeling, how much time you have available, and what the weather's like!

Q: What makes a team successful?

Q: What do you think helps a team work well together?

Q: What kind of groups (clubs, societies etc) do you belong to (or have you in the past)?

Q: What good things did you get out of being in those groups?

Q: Was there a downside?

Q: Why do you think some people like to 'show off' their membership of a particular group?

Q: And why might someone want to conceal it?

## 1 One with God

**Read**

Ephesians 2:1–10

Paul describes two groups of people, those who don't know Jesus (including us in the past) and those who do.

Q: What does Paul say was influencing our behaviour before we knew Jesus?


Q: We all know some people who are still in the first group. What does Paul mean when he says those who don't yet know Jesus are dead?


Q: How is someone saved from this death?


Q: What difference does knowing Jesus make to you?


God's plan – to bring everyone and everything together, with Jesus at the head – begins here, with the reconciliation of God and his people. The plan continues with the reconciliation of God's people to one another.

## 2 One people

**Read**

Ephesians 2:11–22

Q: Who are the two groups Paul writes about here?


Q: What were these two groups like **before** Jesus came along?

Q: What changed for each group **after** Jesus' death?

## reflect

Q: When have you felt like a 'foreigner' or an 'alien'?

Perhaps you've been abroad, surrounded by people speaking a language you didn't understand, perhaps you've started a new job or a new school and found you didn't know anyone and didn't know what to do or where to go.

Q: How did you feel in that situation?

Q: What does it feel like to be on the other side – the one who does know what is going on, who knows they belong?

Paul describes the church as a body (1:23); a temple building (2:21,22) and God's family (2:19). We are an important part of it (2:22).

Q: How do you feel about being a brick in God's building or a member of God's household?

**Reality check** Today's church is still full of people who are very different to each other. Some fit in easily, others may not. There may even be people we really don't like at all. Recently one Anglican diocese issued guidelines for including and accepting someone who was both a convicted paedophile and a Christian believer. The guidelines discussed how such a person could be welcomed as a part of the church family, whilst ensuring that children are safe and the person is protected from temptation. It's an incredibly difficult thing to get right and all sorts of emotions can be stirred up.

Q: Why does the church try to be so inclusive when most other organisations wouldn't consider it?

This is an extreme situation but demonstrates how difficult it is to live as one body. Even though our churches are not divided into Jews and Gentiles, there may still be those who feel like foreigners. These might be:

- the young in a church full of older people
- the sick in a church where everyone seems healthy
- single people in a church with lots of families
- black people in a church where every other face is white

Q: Are there other groups of people who might feel excluded?


Q: Which of these applies to your church?


Q: What one thing could you change, or do better, to help others move from that sense of being a foreigner to being a citizen, a full member of God's family?

- as a whole church?
- as a group?
- as an individual?

Take five minutes of quiet to think through the next few questions on your own, remembering that reconciliation is part of God's purpose for the world.

Q: Are any of your relationships with other people marked by hostility or suspicion?


Q: How could you begin to rebuild your relationship with that person?


Q: Is there something you could decide now to do about it this week?

re:action

## 1 Praying for a nation

**Choose a nation** to pray for as a group – a nation where reconciliation between groups is much needed. Think about how you could find information that would help you to pray more constructively?

- Does someone in your group know someone living or working in that country?
- Can you get hold of a copy of *Operation World*, a publication updated regularly which lists lots of useful data to encourage specific prayer for all the nations of the world? (This book is from OM Publishing of Carlisle, ISBN 1 85078 120 6)
- Could someone volunteer to collect anything about that country that appears in newspapers?
- Could someone research using the Internet?
- Does anyone have other books that might give information or describe the life of people in that country (including fiction)?
- Are there Christian agencies or churches working there that produce prayer leaflets or magazines?
- What other ideas do you have?

Perhaps you could **pray together for that nation** from next session and throughout the time you are studying Ephesians, using information collected by the group.

## 2 Praying for ourselves

It is often easier to pray for a far-away country than to tackle difficulties in our own church or our own lives.

One person could **read** this verse out loud:

*You must make allowance for each other's faults and forgive the person who offends you. Remember, the Lord forgave you, so you must forgive others.*
Colossians 3:13

**Sitting quietly**, allow God to show you who you have hurt who you need to forgive

Using these words or your own, **say a prayer** in your heart, asking forgiveness:

> Lord, forgive me for the hurt I have caused others, knowingly or accidentally. Please give me your strength so I can forgive those who have hurt me. Fill me with the courage and the wisdom I need to take that difficult first step in rebuilding my relationships. May I learn to love others as you love me. Amen.

If you feel able to, you could **tell** the others in your group what you plan to do about these relationships this week. **Ask** them to pray for you now and during the week and then tell them how things went at your next meeting.

# 3 No more secrets

*God himself revealed his secret plan to me.*

**Ephesians 3:3**

## set the scene

Set up a 'hot seat' in the middle of your group and persuade someone to sit in it. You might want to make the hot seat the most comfortable chair available, to encourage them! Allow the volunteer a minute to think of something about themselves that the others don't know. This could be anything: being able to speak fluent Polish, owning all the Steps albums, having a hole in their vest or walking into a bus stop on the way to work this morning… whatever they choose.

Give the rest of the group two minutes to find out what the secret is – but the person in the hot seat can't say anything to guide them except 'yes' and 'no'.

Q: Did you discover their secret, and how quickly?

If you have time, repeat the game with others in the hot seat.

## explore

### 1 Sharing Good News

**Read**

Ephesians 3:1–13

Q: Are you a fan of mystery stories (fictional or real-life)?

Q: What do (or don't) you like about them?

Here Paul talks about another kind of mystery: God's secret plan. This mystery isn't a puzzling event or something with no rational explanation. Instead, this is something that was once hidden but has now been explained to everyone by God, through Paul.

Q: What is the secret plan, or mystery, Paul is talking about?


**Picture it** You're at home on the phone, doodling on a notepad while trying to give the double-glazing salesman a reasonably polite brush-off. Suddenly you realise you've come up with

- a fantastic plan for a non-polluting, cheap and safe form of transport
- the formula for a cure for all forms of cancer
- some other equally vital invention to benefit the whole world

Q: What would be the best thing to do with your discovery? Tick your first choice.

    \_\_\_\_ lose it in a pile of papers

    \_\_\_\_ patent it

    \_\_\_\_ show it to someone who knows about these things

    \_\_\_\_ find someone to put it into production

    \_\_\_\_ something else – what?


Q: Why might it be good to share your great idea with your friends/this group?


Q: Why does Paul share his new understanding of God's plans with us?


## 2 Paul sharing with the Gentiles

Q: What is Paul's message for the Gentiles? (v8)


Q: What do we gain from knowing Jesus? (It will be helpful to look back at chapters 1 and 2)

## 3 Paul sharing with everyone

Q: Who are these rulers and authorities in the heavenly realms?
(v9–11)


**Read**
1 Peter 1:12
Ephesians 6:12

Q: What does Paul say the church is to show them?


Q: How is it going to do this?


## reflect

It's Sunday morning and it's time to go to church.

Q: How do you feel? Why?


**Reality check**  My actions don't just affect my personal relationship
with God or God's work in the world – but have a supernatural effect
too. We aren't intended to live solo lives as Christians, but to take our
place in the Body, being actively involved with the church community.

Q: How should my presence at church make it easier for:
  • my relationship with Jesus to grow?
  • other Christians to grow?
  • the church to reach out into the world?
  • the rulers and authorities to understand God's purposes?

Q: Which of these things are you concentrating on during a Sunday
service?


Q: What could you be more aware of?

Q: How might you have to change your attitude on a Sunday to do this?

The church is God's advertisement in the world and the heavenly realms. Our life together should demonstrate what God wants to achieve in the whole of creation. Being in the church is not something we can be casual about and discard if it doesn't suit us.

Q: Understanding this, how do we respond to someone who says,

- 'I don't go to church but I'm still a Christian.'
- 'The thing that really matters is developing my personal relationship with Jesus. Church is just a nice extra.'
- 'Church is OK, but I'm not getting anything out of it.'

**Reality check** In spite of this, we don't have to feel that everything happening in every part of the worldwide, national or local church is great all the time! In some churches there are people living in unchallenged, deliberate sin; people who only care about the institution and its ritual; those who won't ever put aside their preferences to reach others; and those who seem to encourage division and argument. Even when we are wholehearted in our desire to serve Jesus, the church can still seem boring, irrelevant and generally 'naff' to those both outside and inside! If we feel that, how much more must God, who chose it to reach both the physical and supernatural world? We need God to help us improve things. He hasn't given up on the church (even though parts of it are not listening to him) so why should we?

Q: How should we respond when part (or all) of the church isn't acting as God would want?

Sometimes, the task may seem very daunting. We are conscious that we aren't always much of an advert for Jesus on our own, never mind together. However, Paul prays for God's help to face the challenge.

**Read**
Ephesians 3:14–21

Q: What does Paul pray that his readers will receive?

Q: How will these things help us to be the church?

Imagine you have been given the job of producing an advert for a perfect version of your church. Your brief is not to attract other Christians but people who don't go to any church at all.

Q: What would you want to tell them?

Q: What might attract people who don't know Jesus and have only negative impressions of the church?

If it's something you and the rest of the group would enjoy, pass round paper and pens and encourage people to sketch their own advert for the church, and then discuss the results.

Q: Do your adverts describe events and meetings? Or do they talk about less tangible things such as relationships with one another and with Jesus?

Q: Which do you think are most important? Why?

Q: Which of these things is your church doing well at the moment?

Q: Where does your church need to change or grow?

## re:action

**Choose** one or two areas from the life of your church. What good things do you see happening there? **Give thanks** for those things together. **Pray** for those who are involved or responsible for that area of church life. (If you don't know their needs, why not ask one of them to write some prayer requests down for your group for next time, or even invite them to come along and share them in person?) During the coming week you could **send** small cards to those involved, encouraging them or thanking them for their efforts.

Next, **take** a few minutes of silence to consider your own involvement in the life of your local church (eg youth work, visiting the sick)? **Think** about the good things that are happening there; and the needs.

**Share** some of these things together and **pray** for one another, silently or aloud as you prefer. If you have committed to pray for reconciliation in a particular nation, do it now.

End by **reading** one of Paul's great prayers out loud together:

*I pray that from his glorious, unlimited resources he will give you mighty inner strength through his Holy Spirit. And I pray that Christ will be more and more at home in your hearts as you trust in him. May your roots go down deep into the soil of God's marvellous love. And may you have the power to understand, as all God's people should, how wide, how long, how high, and how deep his love really is. May you experience the love of Christ, though it is so great you will never fully understand it. Then you will be filled with the fullness of life and power that comes from God.*

*Now glory be to God! By his mighty power at work within us, he is able to accomplish infinitely more than we would ever dare to ask or hope. May he be given glory in the church and in Christ Jesus for ever and ever through endless ages. Amen.*

Ephesians 3:16–21

# 4 United we stand

*Under his direction, the whole body is fitted together perfectly.*

**Ephesians 4:16**

## set the scene

Q: What happened on the best birthday you can remember as a child?

Q: Was there a particular age you really wanted to be? Why?

**Imagine it** You're walking down the street with several people walking towards you. Without thinking about it you know which of these people is a child and which is an adult.

Q: How do we tell the difference between children and adults?

**Reality check** Nothing stops a person from growing older but, unfortunately, growing older doesn't automatically bring us greater maturity. We can probably all think of adults who have never grown up; not so much in their interests – a mature person can still like Eeyore or train sets or wearing football shirts – but in their relationships and their attitudes to others.

Q: What kind of things might show that an adult was still immature?

Just as our maturity as people is not directly linked to how old we are, our maturity as Christians is not directly linked to how long we've been a Christian. Being a Christian doesn't mean that we will automatically grow more mature year by year

In his letter to the Ephesians, Paul describes what a mature Christian should be like and why it is so important to go on growing.

explore

**Read**

Ephesians 4:1–6

The first sign of a mature Christian or group of Christians is unity. Our 'oneness' is not based on our church structures but on the way we treat one another.

## 1 Building blocks of unity: humility and gentleness

Q: How much do you agree or disagree with these statements?
**Humble people**
- always put other people's needs first
- downplay their successes and abilities
- let others decide what to do and how to do it
- are rightly seen as a bit 'wet' or 'drippy'

**Gentle people**
- don't disagree with people
- are easily manipulated
- get taken advantage of
- are rightly thought of as 'soft'

Jesus described himself as humble and gentle (Matthew 11:29) and he was certainly not drippy or soft!

**Read**

John 13:12–16
Romans 12:10
Philippians 2:3–7

Q: With these verses in mind, what characteristics would you see in someone who was humble and gentle like Jesus?

**Reality check** Spiritual gentleness has real strength but keeps it under control. Humility was weak and despicable to the Greeks – but Jesus made it the cornerstone of character.

Take a few minutes of quiet to think through the next couple of questions on your own.

Q: How would you score yourself out of 10 for humility? And for gentleness?

Q: What do you need to change or think about to grow more of these characteristics in your life?

Share with the group if you'd like to.

Q: How do these qualities help to build unity in the church?
(Or, if you prefer, how does a lack of them lead to divisions?)

## 2 Building blocks of unity: patience

The stories of Jemima and Flo, of Rebecca and Jenny, of Simon and Basil are told right near the beginning of the book in the Intro section. Check them out if you've not read them or have forgotten all about their tales of differences.

Q: How do you react when people from church

- upset you?
- ignore you?
- step on your toes?
- don't do something they should have done?
- do it but do it wrong?

**Reality check** Unity is built on our behaviour towards each other and on our common beliefs (v2–6). However, it does not result in a group of clones all looking, behaving and feeling alike. Our unity can be strengthened by our diversity, our differences. We all have something different to offer and so all our needs can be met, not by one person but by the Body working properly together.

## 3 Playing my part

**Read**

Ephesians 4:7–16

Paul reminds us that:

- We all have something to offer to the life of the church (v7).
- We all have something different to offer to the life of the church (v11).

Q: What should the leadership of the church be doing (v11,12)?


Everyone has times when they will be receiving from the others in the Body and not serving; perhaps during illness or after first joining a new church. However, most of us, most of the time, are needed to play our God-given part in the Body of Christ, the church (v16).

Often churches (or individuals within them) seem to get this pattern upside-down – the leadership do the work, the congregation receive their efforts.

Q: Which way up is your church?


Q: What are the dangers for a church that works upside-down?


Q: What is our joint life intended to bring about? (v13)


Q: As you develop greater maturity, what benefits does that bring you?


Q: And the church?


reflect

**Read**

Colossians 3:12–14

Q: Are there limits to the amount of patience and forgiveness we should show those around us in church?

Q: When you're upset with someone how often do you:
- moan to others without confronting the person themselves?
- expect someone to change even though they don't know how you feel?
- expect someone to change instantly, totally and permanently?

Earlier you may have read the end of the story of Jesus washing the disciples' feet (John 13:1–17).

Q: What attitude did Jesus show towards the disciples through doing that?

Imagine your church has suddenly been filled with people who have amazingly clean-smelling feet and socks and you are going round washing people's feet...

Q: Are there people who you would find it hard to serve in this way? Why?

And now a question for you to take a few minutes to think about quietly on your own.

Q: What one step could you take to grow in your patience, tolerance and forgiveness of others?

## re:action

Someone from the group could read John 17:20,21:

*I am praying not only for these disciples but also for all who will ever believe in me because of their testimony. My prayer for all of them is that they will be one, just as you and I are one, Father – that just as you are in me and I am in you, so they will be in us, and the world will believe you sent me.*

**Discuss** all the good things you can think of that come from living as one Body.

We are all different from one another and sometimes groups are good at recognising those differences and sometimes they are not.

On your own, **think about** your life at present and **write down** one or two things about your life that make it different from most or all of the others in your group. Think about things such as age, life situation, family, personality, work patterns, health issues etc. Examples might include being unemployed or a single parent or much younger than the others.

My differences
1
2

Now, **share** these with the group, and **tell** them about the one thing you would most like the others in your group to know or understand about how these differences affect you. If you can, **suggest** – in a positive way – ways in which the others can help or support you.

For example, if you're the only unemployed person in a group you might want the others to understand that you don't have enough money to go out for a Christmas meal and would prefer a home-grown meal this year. If you have health problems you might want them to understand that sometimes you can't make a meeting or feel left out if everyone else plans an energetic outing together.

**Pray** together, out loud or silently:
- for forgiveness for times you have hurt other members of your group
- that you will learn to recognise and take account of one another's differences and make every member feel valued
- that the Holy Spirit would be at the centre of your relationships, the glue that binds every member together
- for your relationships to be marked by honesty and love.

Don't forget to **pray** for your 'adopted' nation.

You could end by saying together the blessing that Christians call 'the grace':

*May the grace of our Lord Jesus Christ and the love of God, and the fellowship of the Holy Spirit be with us all, evermore. Amen.*

# 5 Sparkling speech

*You must display a new nature because you are a new person...*

**Ephesians 4:24**

set the scene

Start by playing a round or two of Chinese Whispers – the game where a complicated message is passed round a circle from one person to the next in whispers. If you want to make it slightly more complicated then start two (or more) different messages at once, going in different directions round the group.

Q: What do we learn about communication from playing this game?

explore

**Read**

Ephesians 4:17–5:20

When we become Christians, we put off our old lives and put on our new selves. For all of us that is an ongoing process, but, as we mature, the new self grows and the old shrinks. In this passage Paul discusses the new ways we should speak and act. In this study we focus on speech, next time on actions.

Q: What kinds of speech does Paul say we should put an end to?

Q: And what should we replace it with?

Q: What makes negative speech so destructive to relationships?

# 1 Speaking truthfully

Lying might be said to come in two categories:

- lies of commission – deliberate lies
- lies of omission – leaving out the whole truth

Q: Should a Christian always tell the truth, the whole truth and nothing but the truth?

Q: When – if at all – might it be right to 'modify' or 'postpone' the truth?

*The Message* Bible paraphrase gives Ephesians 4:25 as:

*What this adds up to, then, is this; no more lies, no more pretense. Tell your neighbor the truth. In Christ's body we're all connected to each other, after all. When you lie to others, you end up lying to yourself.*

This isn't just about telling lies – it's also about pretending, presenting a false picture of ourselves.

Q: What kinds of things do we try to hide about ourselves from others? Why?

Q: How does this deception affect our relationships with one another?

Q: How do you deal with someone telling you lies, or presenting a picture of themselves that you know to be false?

Q: How do you deal with someone telling you truth that you do not want to hear?

Q: In what ways could you be more honest with others?

## 2 Encouraging others

Paul's advice and encouragement included this:

*Let everything you say be good and helpful, so that your words will be an encouragement to those who hear them.*

**Ephesians 4:29b**

Or, in the words of *The Message*:

*Say only what helps, each word a gift.*

Q: If we are to be able to encourage others and build them up, what do we need to know about them?

Q: How can we use what we say to encourage someone?

## 3 Controlling our talk

**Read**

Ephesians 5:4

In some quarters of the Christian world, swearing and dubious jokes are seen as ways of showing Christians to be normal people – perhaps alongside being able to get drunk and fiddle our work expenses.

Q: Why is it so important for Christians to cut out swearing?

Q: And dirty jokes?

Think about these two different scenarios.

Bill works in an office where swearing and crude jokes are not just socially acceptable but almost a requirement; it's become standard behaviour in the coffee breaks, around the photocopier, and in the sandwich bar at lunchtimes.

Q: How can Bill behave differently without coming across as a boring weirdo?

Mary spends some time sharing personal needs with Joanna. Another member of their house group comes up to Joanna later and asks, 'How's Mary, then?' Joanna replies, 'Well, she's got some real needs for prayer. She's really struggling with....'

Q: Joanna might claim, 'I don't gossip. I merely pass on prayer needs'. How should Joanna have replied? And what advice could you give her?

Discuss this hard-hitting comment from the Bible, from the book of James:

*Anyone who considers himself religious and does not keep a tight rein on his tongue deceives himself and his religion is worthless*

**James 1:26**

## Stop and think...

Q: Is your group clear about confidentiality?

Q: Are you sure that if someone shared something very personal, it would stay among the members of the group?

Q: Is it OK to share with other members of the group that are missing that night?

Q: What about those that have partners (and families) that aren't in the group? Can they share things with them or not?

Don't assume everyone will behave the same way without discussion. If you haven't ever talked about confidentiality before, maybe now is the time before problems come up.

## reflect

On your own, **think** about these elements of your speech and score yourself against each. Put:

    1  for 'I'm pretty good at this'
    2  'I make the odd slip now and again'
    3  'I need to watch this area'
    4  'Awful'

speaking truthfully                  \_\_\_

doing good to those you talk to    \_\_\_

listening carefully                  \_\_\_

swearing                          \_\_\_

gossip                            \_\_\_

dirty jokes                     \_\_\_

Q: How are you doing?


If you know your group well enough, you might want to share your thoughts.

Q: Which area(s) do you need to work on most?


Q: What one step could you take to start speaking more positively?


Q: Are there people you know your speech has hurt?


Q: What first step could you take to try and put that right?

Part of Christian maturity is being willing to be corrected by others.

Q: How open are you to others telling you when you display less than sparkling speech?

## Re:action

**Brainstorm** the different kinds of ways God speaks to his people – such as promises, commands, comforting words. If you're stuck for where to look, try the Psalms. Have your Bibles open and see if you can **find** some examples. As you discover something, **read it out** to the whole group. **Discuss** how that word from God makes you feel – challenged, encouraged etc.

Spend some time **praying** for each other, using some of the verses that you have found. Include the nation you are praying for – perhaps you could pray one of the verses for the people of that country?

If any of the verses makes an impact on you, **write it down** on a piece of paper and keep it on the fridge door for the next week as a reminder.

# 6 Beautiful behaviour

*Follow God's example in everything you do...*

**Ephesians 5:1**

Q: How was school for you? Tick where it's appropriate.
For me, school was:

____ something to be avoided

____ something to be got through and abandoned as quickly
as possible

____ a means to an end

____ OK in parts

____ endlessly fascinating

____ other – what? _____

Much of the information we learn at school doesn't seem to linger past
our leaving date.

Q: Is there anything you learned in secondary school that is still of
use to you?


Q: Do you see yourself as an enthusiastic learner now or not? What
kind of things do you enjoy learning the most – skills, ideas,
facts...? Why?


**Imagine** You've decided to change career and become a brain
surgeon. You turn up on the first day and you are given a book called
*Ten Easy Steps to Successful Brain Operations*. You're told to go away,
read the book and come back in a week. On your return you find your
first operation begins in two hours – and you're in charge!

Q: What advice would you give your prospective patients?

Saying you are a surgeon or a hairdresser or a pilot doesn't automatically give you the skills to be one.

Q: Why isn't it possible for us to learn these kinds of skills solely from books?

## explore

*Sticks and stones may break my bones
but words will... stay with me forever!*

**Read**

Ephesians 4:22–24

**Reality check** What we say, and how we say it, matters. However, it's possible to say things we don't mean. What we **do** backs up or denies the truth of what we say. Eventually the way you behave, especially in your relationships, displays the real you. Paul tells us to put off the old self and instead put on the new. Our standing in God's eyes changes instantly but our behaviour doesn't change so quickly! Paul encourages us to live in a way that is in keeping with our new relationship with God: live a life worthy of the calling you have received (4:1); and he gives us tips on how to do it.

**Read**

Ephesians 4:32–5:2

Q: How does Paul recommend we should learn about living life?

Q: What two things does Paul particularly expect us to copy?

Q: Does Paul place limits on our imitation? Is it realistic to expect us to behave just like Jesus?

Q: What does following the example of Jesus mean for the way we forgive and love other people?

Paul encourages us to imitate the Master, to look to him for the way to live. He then goes on to give us some tips for keeping on track.

## 1 Top tip for life: Live in the light

### Read

John 3:19–21

Ephesians 4:17–27 and 5:3–14

Through the second half of his letter to the Ephesians, Paul describes the behaviour of those who live in darkness and the changed behaviour of those who live in the light.

Q: What kind of actions does Paul describe in Ephesians 5:11 and what kind of things might he mean?

Q: How can we measure whether our behaviour is a hangover from our previous lifestyles or really 'of the light'?

Q: How does anger give Satan a foothold in our lives? (4:27)

Q: Why does Paul describe the immoral, impure and greedy as idolaters? (5:5)

Q: Why is Paul so opposed even to talking about the details of wrong behaviour? (5:12)

## 2 Top tip for life: Be wise

### Read

Ephesians 5:15–20

Q: What does it mean to live wisely?

Q: How can we learn what his will is?

Q: Why is spiritual wisdom such a great gift to have?

## 3 Top tip for life: Submit to one another

**Read**

Ephesians 5:21–33

Verse 21 is a principle that should apply to all our relationships within the church. Paul describes specific relationships where the principle should (and often isn't) applied but it is for **all** our relationships with our brothers and sisters. Paul doesn't tell us to submit only to those in authority in the church but to one another – to everyone.

Q: What kind of attitudes and feelings do we associate with the idea of submission?

Q: Why might we find the idea of submitting to others in the church difficult?

Q: What are the risks of submitting myself to ordinary, fallible people?

Q: How should I respond to those who submit to me?

Q: How might the principle of submitting to one another affect our behaviour when

- new people come into a morning service?

- someone different arrives in our house group?

## 4 Top tip for life: Have the right attitude to authority

**Read**

Ephesians 6:1–9

Q: How should we obey those in authority over us?

Q: What might this mean for those of us who work for others?

Q: How should we behave towards those who work for us?

Notice that Paul does not make these statements conditional. He doesn't say that we are to obey our masters **as long as** they... We are called to play our part and not worry about what everyone else is doing.

reflect

Living in the light means that we are open to others, and to Jesus, looking at the way we live. When things are going wrong we may be the last to realise it. Sometimes those close to us notice some failings very clearly but miss others as they are so used to them. We may have work colleagues who will comment on our professional failings but rarely on our personal ones.

Q: Why is accountability so important in our relationships within the church family?

Q: If nobody ever 'tells you off' does it mean you're perfect? Or do you need to find someone you can trust to play that role for you and ask them to do it?

Q: What qualities would you look for in that person?

The next few questions are probably best tackled quietly on your own. Think about the people in your church.

Q: Who, outside your immediate family, would you allow to point out that you were behaving badly?

Q: When did someone last do it to you? And how did you feel?

Q: Would you let them do it again? If yes, have you told them so?

Q: What one practical step could you take as a result of this week's study, that would help you to grow further into your new clothes – to live more as God would want you to?

## re:action

One person should be asked to **read out loud** Ephesians 5:15–20 again.

Either on your own or with a partner, **choose** a psalm, hymn or spiritual song that expresses thanksgiving to God in some way. If some or all of the group would enjoy a creative challenge, you might want to take a few minutes to **write** your own prayers or psalms of thanksgiving instead.

**Share** what you have come up with, whether that's something you've written or not. **Read out** the psalms or prayers. **Sing or listen** to the hymns or songs people have chosen.

If your group is too big to use everyone's contribution in one session, hold some of them over for your next meeting and begin with a time of thanksgiving then.

End by **sharing** your 'next steps' in pairs, **praying** together that God will give you the strength, wisdom and opportunity to follow them through. Don't forget to **pray** for the nation you have been bringing before God each week.

# 7 The family at war

*Be strong with the Lord's mighty power.*

**Ephesians 6:10**

## set the scene

Start by playing a version of the **Truth or Lies Game**. Each person thinks of three statements about themselves. Two are true and one is false. In turn, each person tells the others their three statements and the rest of the group have to decide which one they think is false.

Q: During the game, how did you try to work out which statement was false?

Q: What would make this task easier for you?

## explore

### 1 You're in the army now!

*This is no afternoon athletic contest that we'll walk away from and forget about in a couple of hours.This is for keeps, a life-or-death fight to the finish against the Devil and all his angels.*

**Ephesians 6:12** *The Message*

**Read**

Ephesians 6:10–24

Q: How does the Intelligence Corps help an army in wartime?

Q: Who is the Christian's enemy?

**Read**

Ephesians 6:12
1 Peter 5:8,9
John 8:44
Matthew 4:3
2 Corinthians 11:14,15
James 4:7

Q: What is the enemy like?


Q: God created Satan (and all the angels). What limits does this place on Satan?


Some people dismiss the devil as a figment of the imagination – a childish fantasy. Others imagine him as ever-present, hiding behind every bush.

Q: What are the dangers of under-estimating an enemy?


Q: Is a fear of Satan a healthy attitude or not?


This battle is a partnership. God doesn't do all the work and neither do we. God provides the power; we depend on it to stand firm.

## 2 Preparing the defences

For many Christians the main battle against Satan takes place in their mind. We don't usually experience physical attacks but instead find our attitudes and our relationships with others and with God being disrupted. If Satan can get away with encouraging us to slide into compromise and sin then he will.

Q: What happens to an army only equipped with longbows when their opponents have tanks?

*Truth, righteousness, peace, faith and salvation are more than words. Learn how to apply them. You'll need them throughout your life. God's Word is an indispensable weapon. In the same way, prayer is essential in this ongoing warfare.*

**Ephesians 6:14,15** *The Message*

Our weapons are specifically designed to meet the attacks we will face – no mismatches here.

Q: What kinds of attack do we face? (v16)


Q: Can you think of times when you have faced these kinds of attack?


Q: How did you respond?


We don't need to get up and put the armour on afresh each day; we should be wearing it all the time. We don't want to face surprise attacks unprotected.

Q: Why is the sword – God's truth – such an indispensable protection from attack?


## 3 A key weapon

**Reality check** It could be argued that most victorious armies have one weapon that finally tips the balance in their favour; tanks in the First World War, nuclear weapons in the Second. For us it is prayer – the energy to wield the sword and wear the armour.

Here we have Paul's mini-guide to using prayer effectively (v18):

## a Pray in the Spirit

Q: Is it possible for us to pray any other way?


Q: How can we be sure we are praying in the Spirit?

## b Pray on all occasions

Q: Do you tend to pray before you do – or do before you pray?

Q: What are the benefits of praying first?

## c Pray making all kinds of prayers and requests

Q: Are you creative in your personal prayers? Or do you stick to the same patterns of content, place, position, order... all, or most of, the time?

Q: Together, come up with a list of different ideas for personal prayer – perhaps things you've tried yourself or things you've read or heard about others trying. Sometime this week why not have a go at one or two of the ideas that you've not tried before.

## d Keep on praying for other Christians

*Keep each other's spirits up so that no one falls behind or drops out.*
**Ephesians 6:18** *The Message*

We have a responsibility to pray for one another within the church but we can't easily pray for everyone – except in very general ways. However, we should be praying for some people regularly, perhaps not all of them every day but at least once a week.

Q: How can you decide who to pray for in particular, out of all the people in your church?

Q: How often do you think you should pray for them?

Q: How can you keep up-to-date with their needs?
On you own, make a list of the people in your church that you should be praying for.

re:action

Q: Would it help them if you told them you were praying for them?

## e Ask people to pray (v19)

Q: When did you last ask someone to pray for a real need you had?

reflect

Be prepared! Satan searches for an unguarded area to use as a beach-head (see 4:27). If there are chinks in your armour, he will find them.

Q: What kinds of things might weaken our defences?

**Reality check** Satan does not want us to know God's blessing and will do what he can to obstruct our growth, rob us of what we have learned and push us back from serving in ministry.

Q: Can you see where Satan is trying to undermine your growth?
Some clues to answering this:
  • Are you conscious of being pulled into sin?
  • Are things getting in the way of true priorities?
  • Is a relationship suffering?
  • Are you coasting in your ministry?

Whether we are experiencing these attacks now or not, we need to be prepared for them.

Q: How can you prepare and strengthen yourself now against future attacks?

Our enemy is already defeated and eventually we will see that victory. Until that time we fight to claim that victory for ourselves.

Paul said that we should encourage one another in the challenges of being a Christian (6:21,22).

Q: Why does it help us to speak to one another about our Christian lives?

## To recap:

- God chose you to be one of his children, and to be part of the process of bringing the world to know him.
- God brings his people together as the church, as his presence on earth and as a witness to the angels.
- We are called to be distinctively different in our lifestyles; living in unity; playing our part in the church; living holy lives in speech and behaviour and submitted to one another.
- We are called to stand firm in the battle against Satan, strong in God's power.

Q: Which of these points – or any others covered in these sessions – has been most meaningful or helpful to you?

## Re:action

At the end of the **Preview** session, you prayed that everyone in the group might grow in their knowledge of God (Ephesians 1:17). If this has happened to you, **tell** the rest of the group, and **describe** how. After as many people as want to have shared their experiences on this, each person could **pray** a one-sentence prayer of thanks to God.

Talk over future plans for the group. Are you continuing to meet, with new materials to guide your discussions and study? Or taking a break and re-forming as a group later?

End by **reading** Ephesians 6:23, 24 together:

*May God give you peace, dear brothers and sisters, and love with faith, from God the Father and the Lord Jesus Christ. May God's grace be upon all who love our Lord Jesus Christ with an undying love.*

## Re:action small group Bible resources by Kate Hayes

## Others in the series

### Jesus: the sequel
*Is he really coming back?*
Appointments, schedules, timetables ... we live in a time-bound society. It's so easy to live just for the present. Are you ready for the future? Not just your next career move... your next property... your next set of wheels... or even your plans for retirement. But the future that begins when Jesus himself returns!
**ISBN 1 85999 621 3**

### For the tough times
*Does God care when I'm hurting?*
Whether it's thousands killed in a terrorist attack as you watch on TV, your next door neighbour on chemo for cancer, or your best friend's marriage on shaky ground ... there's no escaping the issue of suffering. Maybe you want to shout at God that's it's just so unfair! Just what's it all for?
**ISBN 1 85999 622 1**

### The possibility of purpose
*What's the meaning of my life?*
A treadmill existence of deadlines and pressures? Or a kaleidoscope of amazing opportunities? What's your take on daily life? Do you see yourself as a meaningless cosmic dust speck? Or a significant mover in a masterplan? Your view affects your motivation, your self-esteem, your priorities, your everyday choices...
**ISBN 1 85999 620 5**

**Available from all good Christian bookshops**
- phone SU's mail order line: 01908 856006
- email info@scriptureunion.org.uk
- fax 01908 856020
- log on to www.scriptureunion.org.uk
- or write to SU Mail Order:
  PO Box 5148, Milton Keynes MLO, MK2 2YX